AF234605

Scruffy Ted
gets lost

Story written by Karra McFarlane
Illustrated by John Solomon

"I have lost Scruffy Ted,"
Meg tells Gran.

"Will you help?"

Gran picks up a blanket from Fluff the kitten's bed. Meg checks the bed.

Scruffy Ted is not in the kitten's bed.

Gran lifts the lid off a pink box.
Meg checks the box.

Scruffy Ted is not in the box.

Gran tips up a basket. Meg checks the basket.

Scruffy Ted is not in the basket. It is filled with stuff!

Retell the story

Take turns retelling the story with your child.